50 Dairy-Free Chocolate Making Recipes for Home

By: Kelly Johnson

Table of Contents

- Dairy-Free Dark Chocolate Truffles
- Vegan Chocolate Fudge
- Coconut Oil Chocolate Bark
- Dairy-Free Chocolate Covered Almonds
- Vegan Chocolate Mousse
- Dairy-Free Chocolate Banana Bread
- Almond Butter Chocolate Cups
- Dairy-Free Chocolate Coconut Bars
- Vegan Chocolate Chip Cookies
- Chocolate Avocado Pudding
- Dairy-Free Chocolate Hazelnut Spread
- Vegan Chocolate Cherry Brownies
- Dairy-Free Chocolate Zucchini Bread
- Chocolate Chia Seed Pudding
- Dairy-Free Chocolate Covered Strawberries
- Vegan Chocolate Peanut Butter Cups
- Dairy-Free Chocolate Popsicles
- Chocolate Covered Dates
- Vegan Chocolate Cheesecake
- Dairy-Free Chocolate Coconut Milkshake
- Chocolate Quinoa Breakfast Bowl
- Dairy-Free Chocolate Protein Balls
- Vegan Chocolate Raspberry Tart
- Dairy-Free Chocolate Cherry Smoothie
- Chocolate Banana Nice Cream
- Vegan Chocolate Granola Bars
- Dairy-Free Chocolate Oatmeal Cookies
- Chocolate Coconut Bliss Balls
- Vegan Chocolate Espresso Cake
- Dairy-Free Chocolate Avocado Smoothie Bowl
- Chocolate Hazelnut Energy Bites
- Vegan Chocolate Chia Pudding Parfait
- Dairy-Free Chocolate Peppermint Patties
- Chocolate Almond Butter Energy Bars
- Vegan Chocolate Pumpkin Bread

- Dairy-Free Chocolate Coconut Ice Cream
- Chocolate Almond Milkshake
- Vegan Chocolate Coconut Flour Pancakes
- Dairy-Free Chocolate Raspberry Popsicles
- Chocolate Peanut Butter Rice Krispie Treats
- Vegan Chocolate Caramel Slice
- Dairy-Free Chocolate Macaroons
- Chocolate Cherry Smoothie Bowl
- Vegan Chocolate Zucchini Muffins
- Dairy-Free Chocolate Almond Milk Pudding
- Chocolate Banana Chia Seed Pudding Parfait
- Vegan Chocolate Orange Cake
- Dairy-Free Chocolate Peanut Butter Smoothie
- Chocolate Coconut Chia Seed Pudding
- Vegan Chocolate Black Bean Brownies

Dairy-Free Dark Chocolate Truffles

Ingredients:

- 8 ounces dairy-free dark chocolate, finely chopped
- 1/2 cup full-fat coconut milk
- 1 teaspoon vanilla extract
- Cocoa powder, shredded coconut, chopped nuts, or powdered sugar for rolling (optional)

Instructions:

Prepare the chocolate: Place the finely chopped dairy-free dark chocolate in a heatproof bowl.

Heat the coconut milk: In a small saucepan, heat the coconut milk over medium heat until it just begins to simmer. Do not let it come to a boil.

Combine ingredients: Pour the hot coconut milk over the chopped chocolate. Let it sit for 1-2 minutes to soften the chocolate. Then, add the vanilla extract.

Stir until smooth: Gently stir the chocolate and coconut milk mixture until the chocolate is completely melted and the mixture is smooth and well combined.

Chill the mixture: Cover the bowl and refrigerate the mixture for about 1-2 hours, or until it firms up and is easy to handle.

Shape the truffles: Once the chocolate mixture has chilled and firmed up, use a small spoon or a melon baller to scoop out portions of the mixture. Roll each portion into a ball between your palms to form truffles. If the mixture becomes too soft to handle, you can briefly chill it again in the refrigerator.

Roll in coatings (optional): If desired, roll the truffles in cocoa powder, shredded coconut, chopped nuts, or powdered sugar to coat them. This step is optional but adds texture and flavor to the truffles.

Chill until set: Place the rolled truffles on a baking sheet lined with parchment paper and refrigerate for another 15-30 minutes, or until they are firm.

Serve: Once the truffles are chilled and set, transfer them to an airtight container and store them in the refrigerator until ready to serve.

Enjoy these delicious Dairy-Free Dark Chocolate Truffles as a decadent treat or gift them to friends and family!

Vegan Chocolate Fudge

Ingredients:

- 1 cup dairy-free chocolate chips
- 1/2 cup creamy almond butter (or any other nut or seed butter of your choice)
- 1/4 cup maple syrup (or agave syrup)
- 1 teaspoon vanilla extract
- Pinch of salt
- Optional toppings: chopped nuts, shredded coconut, sea salt flakes

Instructions:

Prepare the chocolate: In a microwave-safe bowl or a small saucepan, melt the dairy-free chocolate chips until smooth. You can do this by microwaving in 30-second intervals, stirring in between, or by using a double boiler method on the stovetop. Be careful not to overheat the chocolate.

Combine ingredients: Once the chocolate is melted, stir in the creamy almond butter, maple syrup, vanilla extract, and a pinch of salt. Mix until all ingredients are well combined and smooth.

Pour into a pan: Line an 8x8 inch square baking pan with parchment paper, leaving some overhang on the sides for easy removal later. Pour the chocolate mixture into the prepared pan and spread it out evenly with a spatula.

Add toppings (optional): If desired, sprinkle chopped nuts, shredded coconut, or sea salt flakes over the top of the fudge mixture and gently press them down with the back of a spoon or your fingers.

Chill until set: Place the pan in the refrigerator and chill the fudge for at least 2-3 hours, or until it is firm and set.

Slice and serve: Once the fudge is completely chilled and set, use the parchment paper overhang to lift it out of the pan. Transfer it to a cutting board and slice it into squares or rectangles using a sharp knife.

Store: Store the vegan chocolate fudge in an airtight container in the refrigerator for up to two weeks. You can also freeze it for longer storage, if desired.

Enjoy this creamy and indulgent Vegan Chocolate Fudge as a sweet treat or a homemade gift for friends and family!

Coconut Oil Chocolate Bark

Ingredients:

- 1 cup coconut oil
- 1/2 cup cocoa powder (unsweetened)
- 1/4 cup maple syrup or agave nectar
- 1 teaspoon vanilla extract
- Pinch of salt
- Optional toppings: shredded coconut, chopped nuts, dried fruit, sea salt flakes

Instructions:

Prepare a baking sheet: Line a baking sheet with parchment paper or a silicone baking mat. Set aside.

Melt the coconut oil: In a medium saucepan, melt the coconut oil over low heat until it becomes liquid.

Combine ingredients: Once the coconut oil is melted, whisk in the cocoa powder, maple syrup or agave nectar, vanilla extract, and a pinch of salt. Continue to whisk until the mixture is smooth and well combined.

Pour onto the baking sheet: Pour the chocolate mixture onto the prepared baking sheet. Use a spatula to spread it out into an even layer, about 1/4 to 1/2 inch thick.

Add toppings (optional): Sprinkle your desired toppings over the chocolate bark while it's still warm. This could include shredded coconut, chopped nuts, dried fruit, or a sprinkle of sea salt flakes for a sweet and salty contrast.

Chill: Place the baking sheet in the refrigerator and chill the chocolate bark for at least 1-2 hours, or until it is completely set and firm.

Break into pieces: Once the chocolate bark is firm, remove it from the refrigerator and use your hands or a knife to break it into smaller pieces.

Serve: Serve the coconut oil chocolate bark immediately, or store it in an airtight container in the refrigerator for up to two weeks.

Enjoy your delicious Coconut Oil Chocolate Bark as a tasty treat or homemade gift!

Dairy-Free Chocolate Covered Almonds

Ingredients:

- 1 cup whole almonds
- 1 cup dairy-free chocolate chips (such as Enjoy Life or Pascha brands)
- Optional: 1 teaspoon coconut oil (for a smoother chocolate coating)
- Optional toppings: sea salt, shredded coconut, cocoa powder, etc.

Instructions:

Toast the almonds (optional): Preheat your oven to 350°F (175°C). Spread the almonds evenly on a baking sheet and toast them in the oven for about 8-10 minutes, or until they become fragrant and slightly golden. Remove from the oven and let them cool.

Prepare a baking sheet: Line a baking sheet with parchment paper or a silicone baking mat. This will prevent the chocolate-covered almonds from sticking.

Melt the chocolate: In a microwave-safe bowl, melt the dairy-free chocolate chips in 30-second intervals, stirring in between each interval, until the chocolate is completely melted and smooth. Alternatively, you can melt the chocolate using a double boiler on the stovetop. If you want a smoother chocolate coating, stir in a teaspoon of coconut oil until fully combined.

Coat the almonds: Once the chocolate is melted and smooth, add the almonds to the bowl of melted chocolate. Use a spoon or fork to coat each almond completely in chocolate, then remove them one by one, tapping off any excess chocolate.

Place on the baking sheet: Transfer each chocolate-covered almond to the prepared baking sheet, spacing them out so they don't touch each other. This will allow them to cool and harden without sticking together.

Optional toppings: If you want to add any toppings such as sea salt, shredded coconut, or cocoa powder, sprinkle them over the chocolate-covered almonds while the chocolate is still wet.

Chill: Place the baking sheet in the refrigerator for about 20-30 minutes, or until the chocolate has completely hardened.

Serve or store: Once the chocolate has hardened, you can serve the dairy-free chocolate-covered almonds immediately, or transfer them to an airtight container and store them in the refrigerator for later enjoyment.

Enjoy your delicious dairy-free chocolate-covered almonds!

Vegan Chocolate Mousse

Ingredients:

- 1 can (13.5 oz or 400ml) full-fat coconut milk, chilled in the refrigerator overnight
- 8 oz (about 230g) vegan dark chocolate chips or chopped dark chocolate
- 1-2 tablespoons maple syrup or agave syrup (adjust to taste)
- 1 teaspoon vanilla extract
- Optional toppings: fresh berries, shaved chocolate, coconut whipped cream, etc.

Instructions:

Chill the coconut milk: Place the can of coconut milk in the refrigerator overnight. This will cause the coconut milk to separate, with the thick coconut cream rising to the top.
Melt the chocolate: In a microwave-safe bowl or using a double boiler, melt the vegan dark chocolate until smooth. Allow it to cool slightly.
Prepare the coconut cream: Remove the chilled coconut milk from the refrigerator. Open the can and scoop out the thick coconut cream that has risen to the top, leaving behind any watery liquid at the bottom. Place the coconut cream in a separate mixing bowl.
Whip the coconut cream: Using a hand mixer or a stand mixer fitted with the whisk attachment, whip the coconut cream on high speed until it becomes light and fluffy, resembling whipped cream.
Combine with chocolate: Gradually fold the melted chocolate into the whipped coconut cream until fully incorporated. Add maple syrup or agave syrup to sweeten, and vanilla extract for flavor. Taste and adjust sweetness if necessary.
Chill: Transfer the vegan chocolate mousse to serving dishes or glasses. Cover and refrigerate for at least 2-3 hours, or until set.
Serve: Once chilled and set, you can serve the vegan chocolate mousse as is or garnish with your favorite toppings such as fresh berries, shaved chocolate, or coconut whipped cream.
Enjoy: Enjoy this creamy and indulgent vegan chocolate mousse as a delightful dessert!

This recipe is not only dairy-free and vegan but also rich, creamy, and satisfying—a perfect treat for chocolate lovers.

Dairy-Free Chocolate Banana Bread

Ingredients:

- 2 ripe bananas, mashed
- 1/3 cup melted coconut oil (or any other vegetable oil of your choice)
- 1/2 cup coconut sugar (or brown sugar)
- 1 teaspoon vanilla extract
- 1 1/2 cups all-purpose flour
- 1/4 cup unsweetened cocoa powder
- 1 teaspoon baking soda
- 1/2 teaspoon salt
- 1/2 cup dairy-free chocolate chips (optional)
- Chopped nuts (optional)

Instructions:

Preheat your oven to 350°F (175°C). Grease a 9x5-inch loaf pan or line it with parchment paper.
In a large mixing bowl, combine the mashed bananas, melted coconut oil, coconut sugar, and vanilla extract. Mix until well combined.
In a separate bowl, sift together the flour, cocoa powder, baking soda, and salt.
Gradually add the dry ingredients to the wet ingredients, stirring until just combined. Be careful not to overmix.
Fold in the dairy-free chocolate chips and chopped nuts if using, reserving a few to sprinkle on top.
Pour the batter into the prepared loaf pan, spreading it evenly. Sprinkle the remaining chocolate chips and nuts on top.
Bake in the preheated oven for 50-60 minutes, or until a toothpick inserted into the center comes out clean.
Remove the bread from the oven and allow it to cool in the pan for about 10 minutes before transferring it to a wire rack to cool completely.
Once cooled, slice and serve. Enjoy your dairy-free chocolate banana bread!

Feel free to adjust the sweetness according to your taste preferences. You can also add other mix-ins like shredded coconut or dried fruit for extra flavor and texture.

Almond Butter Chocolate Cups

Ingredients:

- 1 cup dairy-free chocolate chips
- 1/4 cup almond butter (or any nut or seed butter of your choice)
- Optional: pinch of salt, vanilla extract, honey or maple syrup for sweetness (if desired)
- Optional toppings: sea salt flakes, chopped nuts, shredded coconut, dried fruit, or extra melted chocolate for drizzling

Instructions:

Prepare your chocolate: Melt the dairy-free chocolate chips in a microwave-safe bowl in 30-second intervals, stirring in between until smooth. Alternatively, you can melt them using a double boiler.
Line a mini muffin tin with mini muffin liners.
Spoon a small amount of melted chocolate into each muffin liner, just enough to cover the bottom.
Place the muffin tin in the freezer for about 10 minutes to set the chocolate.
While the chocolate sets, mix the almond butter with any desired additional ingredients like a pinch of salt, vanilla extract, or sweetener if using.
Once the chocolate has set, remove the muffin tin from the freezer. Spoon a small dollop of almond butter onto the center of each chocolate base.
Cover the almond butter with another layer of melted chocolate, making sure to spread it out to the edges to completely encase the almond butter.
Optional: Sprinkle your desired toppings onto the top layer of chocolate.
Place the muffin tin back in the freezer for another 10-15 minutes, or until the chocolate cups are completely set.
Once set, remove the almond butter chocolate cups from the muffin tin and store them in an airtight container in the refrigerator.
Serve chilled and enjoy your delicious almond butter chocolate cups!

Feel free to experiment with different nut or seed butters, flavorings, and toppings to customize your chocolate cups to your liking. These treats also make wonderful gifts or party favors!

Dairy-Free Chocolate Coconut Bars

Ingredients:

- 2 cups shredded coconut (unsweetened)
- 1/4 cup coconut oil, melted
- 1/4 cup maple syrup or agave nectar
- 1 teaspoon vanilla extract
- 1/4 teaspoon salt
- 1 cup dairy-free chocolate chips

Instructions:

Prepare the coconut mixture:
- In a mixing bowl, combine the shredded coconut, melted coconut oil, maple syrup or agave nectar, vanilla extract, and salt. Stir until well combined.

Press the mixture into a pan:
- Line an 8x8 inch (or similar size) baking pan with parchment paper, leaving some overhang on the sides for easy removal later.
- Transfer the coconut mixture into the lined pan and press it down firmly and evenly using a spatula or the back of a spoon. Make sure to pack it tightly.

Chill the coconut layer:
- Place the pan in the refrigerator for about 30 minutes to firm up the coconut layer.

Prepare the chocolate topping:
- In a microwave-safe bowl or using a double boiler, melt the dairy-free chocolate chips until smooth, stirring occasionally.

Pour the melted chocolate over the coconut layer:
- Once the coconut layer has firmed up, remove the pan from the refrigerator.
- Pour the melted chocolate evenly over the coconut layer, using a spatula to spread it out to the edges and smooth the surface.

Chill until set:
- Return the pan to the refrigerator and chill for another 1-2 hours, or until the chocolate layer is completely set.

Slice and serve:
- Once the chocolate layer has set, remove the pan from the refrigerator.

- Use the parchment paper overhang to lift the chocolate coconut slab out of the pan and transfer it to a cutting board.
- Use a sharp knife to cut the slab into bars or squares of your desired size.

Store and enjoy:
- Store the dairy-free chocolate coconut bars in an airtight container in the refrigerator for up to 1 week.
- Enjoy them chilled straight from the fridge as a tasty snack or dessert!

Feel free to customize these bars by adding chopped nuts, dried fruit, or a sprinkle of sea salt on top of the chocolate layer before it sets. Enjoy your dairy-free chocolate coconut bars!

Vegan Chocolate Chip Cookies

Ingredients:

- 1/2 cup vegan butter, softened (such as Earth Balance)
- 1/2 cup packed brown sugar
- 1/4 cup granulated sugar
- 1 teaspoon vanilla extract
- 2 tablespoons unsweetened applesauce (acts as an egg substitute)
- 1 1/2 cups all-purpose flour
- 1/2 teaspoon baking soda
- 1/2 teaspoon salt
- 1 cup dairy-free chocolate chips

Instructions:

Preheat your oven to 350°F (175°C). Line a baking sheet with parchment paper or silicone baking mat.

In a large mixing bowl, cream together the softened vegan butter, brown sugar, and granulated sugar until light and fluffy.

Add the vanilla extract and unsweetened applesauce to the creamed mixture, and mix until well combined. The applesauce acts as an egg substitute to help bind the dough together.

In a separate bowl, whisk together the all-purpose flour, baking soda, and salt. Gradually add the dry ingredients to the wet ingredients, mixing until a dough forms. Be careful not to overmix.

Fold in the dairy-free chocolate chips until evenly distributed throughout the dough.

Scoop the dough using a tablespoon or cookie scoop, and place the dough balls onto the prepared baking sheet, spacing them about 2 inches apart.

Optional: Gently press down on each dough ball with the back of a spoon or your fingers to slightly flatten them.

Bake in the preheated oven for 10-12 minutes, or until the edges are lightly golden brown. The centers may still look slightly soft, but they will continue to set as they cool.

Remove the cookies from the oven and allow them to cool on the baking sheet for a few minutes before transferring them to a wire rack to cool completely.

Once cooled, serve and enjoy your delicious vegan chocolate chip cookies!

These cookies are perfect for enjoying with a glass of dairy-free milk or sharing with friends and family. Feel free to customize them by adding chopped nuts, dried fruit, or even a sprinkle of sea salt on top before baking. Enjoy!

Chocolate Avocado Pudding

Ingredients:

- 2 ripe avocados
- 1/4 cup cocoa powder (unsweetened)
- 1/4 cup maple syrup or agave nectar (adjust to taste)
- 1/4 cup almond milk (or any other non-dairy milk)
- 1 teaspoon vanilla extract
- Pinch of salt
- Optional toppings: sliced berries, shredded coconut, chopped nuts, or dairy-free whipped cream

Instructions:

Prepare the avocados:
- Cut the avocados in half and remove the pits. Scoop out the flesh and place it in a blender or food processor.

Add the remaining ingredients:
- To the blender or food processor with the avocado, add the cocoa powder, maple syrup or agave nectar, almond milk, vanilla extract, and a pinch of salt.

Blend until smooth:
- Blend all the ingredients together until you have a smooth and creamy pudding-like consistency. You may need to stop and scrape down the sides of the blender or food processor a few times to ensure everything is well incorporated.

Adjust sweetness:
- Taste the pudding and adjust the sweetness to your liking by adding more maple syrup or agave nectar if desired.

Chill the pudding:
- Transfer the chocolate avocado pudding to serving dishes or a bowl. Cover and refrigerate for at least 30 minutes to allow it to chill and firm up slightly.

Serve and enjoy:
- Once chilled, serve the chocolate avocado pudding topped with your favorite toppings such as sliced berries, shredded coconut, chopped nuts, or dairy-free whipped cream.

Store any leftovers in an airtight container in the refrigerator for up to 2 days.

This chocolate avocado pudding is not only delicious but also packed with healthy fats and nutrients from the avocado. It's a great guilt-free dessert option for any occasion!

Dairy-Free Chocolate Hazelnut Spread

Ingredients:

- 2 cups raw hazelnuts
- 1/3 cup cocoa powder (unsweetened)
- 1/2 cup powdered sugar (or adjust to taste)
- 1/4 cup coconut oil, melted
- 1 teaspoon vanilla extract
- Pinch of salt

Instructions:

Roast the hazelnuts:
- Preheat your oven to 350°F (175°C). Spread the hazelnuts evenly on a baking sheet and roast them in the preheated oven for about 10-12 minutes, or until they become fragrant and the skins start to crack.

Remove the skins:
- Once roasted, transfer the hazelnuts to a clean kitchen towel. Fold the towel over the hazelnuts and rub them vigorously to remove as much of the skins as possible. It's okay if some skins remain.

Make the hazelnut butter:
- Once the skins are mostly removed, transfer the hazelnuts to a food processor. Process them for several minutes, scraping down the sides as needed, until they form a smooth and creamy hazelnut butter. This process may take some time, and the hazelnuts will go through various stages, from chopped to ground to finally becoming creamy butter.

Add the remaining ingredients:
- Once you have smooth hazelnut butter, add the cocoa powder, powdered sugar, melted coconut oil, vanilla extract, and a pinch of salt to the food processor.

Blend until smooth:
- Process all the ingredients together until well combined and you have a creamy chocolate hazelnut spread. You may need to scrape down the sides of the food processor occasionally to ensure everything is evenly mixed.

Taste and adjust:
- Taste the chocolate hazelnut spread and adjust the sweetness or saltiness to your liking by adding more powdered sugar or salt if necessary.

Transfer to a jar:
- Once you're happy with the flavor and consistency, transfer the dairy-free chocolate hazelnut spread to a clean, airtight jar or container.

Store and enjoy:
- Store the chocolate hazelnut spread at room temperature for immediate use, or in the refrigerator for longer shelf life. It should keep well for up to 2 weeks.

Enjoy your homemade dairy-free chocolate hazelnut spread on toast, pancakes, waffles, or as a dip for fruit. It's a delicious and healthier alternative to store-bought spreads!

Vegan Chocolate Cherry Brownies

Ingredients:

- 1 cup all-purpose flour
- 3/4 cup cocoa powder (unsweetened)
- 1 teaspoon baking powder
- 1/2 teaspoon baking soda
- 1/2 teaspoon salt
- 1 cup granulated sugar
- 1/2 cup almond milk (or any other non-dairy milk)
- 1/2 cup vegetable oil (such as canola or coconut oil)
- 1 teaspoon vanilla extract
- 1/2 cup dairy-free chocolate chips
- 1 cup fresh or frozen cherries, pitted and halved

Instructions:

Preheat your oven to 350°F (175°C). Grease an 8x8 inch baking pan or line it with parchment paper.

In a large mixing bowl, sift together the all-purpose flour, cocoa powder, baking powder, baking soda, and salt.

In another bowl, whisk together the granulated sugar, almond milk, vegetable oil, and vanilla extract until well combined.

Gradually add the wet ingredients to the dry ingredients, stirring until just combined. Be careful not to overmix.

Fold in the dairy-free chocolate chips and halved cherries until evenly distributed throughout the batter.

Pour the batter into the prepared baking pan, spreading it out evenly with a spatula.

Bake in the preheated oven for 25-30 minutes, or until a toothpick inserted into the center comes out with a few moist crumbs.

Remove the brownies from the oven and allow them to cool in the pan for at least 10-15 minutes before transferring them to a wire rack to cool completely.

Once cooled, slice the brownies into squares and serve. Enjoy your vegan chocolate cherry brownies!

These brownies are best enjoyed fresh, but you can store any leftovers in an airtight container at room temperature for up to 3 days. The combination of chocolate and cherries makes for a decadent and satisfying treat that's perfect for any occasion!

Dairy-Free Chocolate Zucchini Bread

Ingredients:

- 1 1/2 cups grated zucchini (about 1 medium zucchini)
- 1 cup all-purpose flour
- 1/2 cup unsweetened cocoa powder
- 1 teaspoon baking soda
- 1/2 teaspoon baking powder
- 1/4 teaspoon salt
- 1/2 cup granulated sugar
- 1/2 cup brown sugar, packed
- 1/3 cup vegetable oil
- 2 teaspoons vanilla extract
- 2 flax eggs (2 tablespoons ground flaxseed mixed with 6 tablespoons water)
- 1/2 cup dairy-free chocolate chips (optional)

Instructions:

Preheat your oven to 350°F (175°C). Grease a 9x5-inch loaf pan or line it with parchment paper.

Grate the zucchini using a box grater or a food processor. Squeeze out excess moisture from the grated zucchini using a clean kitchen towel or paper towels.

In a large bowl, whisk together the flour, cocoa powder, baking soda, baking powder, and salt until well combined.

In another bowl, mix together the granulated sugar, brown sugar, vegetable oil, vanilla extract, and flax eggs until smooth.

Add the grated zucchini to the wet ingredients and stir until evenly combined.

Gradually add the dry ingredients to the wet ingredients, mixing until just combined. Be careful not to overmix.

Fold in the dairy-free chocolate chips if using.

Pour the batter into the prepared loaf pan and spread it out evenly.

Bake in the preheated oven for 50-60 minutes, or until a toothpick inserted into the center comes out clean.

Allow the bread to cool in the pan for about 10 minutes, then transfer it to a wire rack to cool completely before slicing.

Enjoy your dairy-free chocolate zucchini bread!

Chocolate Chia Seed Pudding

Ingredients:

- 1/4 cup chia seeds
- 1 cup dairy-free milk (such as almond milk, coconut milk, or soy milk)
- 2 tablespoons cocoa powder
- 2-3 tablespoons maple syrup or other sweetener of choice
- 1/2 teaspoon vanilla extract
- Optional toppings: sliced fruits, nuts, coconut flakes, chocolate chips

Instructions:

In a mixing bowl or a jar, combine the chia seeds, cocoa powder, dairy-free milk, maple syrup, and vanilla extract. Stir well to combine all the ingredients thoroughly.

Once well combined, cover the mixture and refrigerate it for at least 4 hours or overnight. This allows the chia seeds to absorb the liquid and thicken the pudding.

After the pudding has set, give it a good stir to break up any clumps and ensure a smooth consistency.

Taste the pudding and adjust the sweetness if necessary by adding more maple syrup or sweetener of your choice.

Serve the chocolate chia seed pudding in individual bowls or glasses.

Optionally, top the pudding with your favorite toppings such as sliced fruits, nuts, coconut flakes, or chocolate chips for added flavor and texture.

Enjoy your delicious and nutritious chocolate chia seed pudding as a satisfying dessert or snack!

This recipe is versatile, so feel free to adjust the sweetness and consistency according to your preference. It's also a great make-ahead option for a quick and healthy treat.

Dairy-Free Chocolate Covered Strawberries

Ingredients:

- Fresh strawberries, washed and dried thoroughly
- Dairy-free chocolate chips or dairy-free chocolate bar (such as dark chocolate)
- Optional toppings: shredded coconut, chopped nuts, sea salt

Instructions:

Line a baking sheet with parchment paper or wax paper.

In a microwave-safe bowl or using a double boiler, melt the dairy-free chocolate chips or chopped dairy-free chocolate bar until smooth and completely melted. If using a microwave, heat the chocolate in 30-second intervals, stirring between each interval until melted.

Once the chocolate is melted and smooth, hold a strawberry by the stem and dip it into the melted chocolate, swirling to coat it completely. Allow any excess chocolate to drip off.

Place the chocolate-covered strawberry onto the prepared baking sheet. Repeat the process with the remaining strawberries.

If desired, sprinkle the tops of the chocolate-covered strawberries with optional toppings such as shredded coconut, chopped nuts, or a pinch of sea salt.

Place the baking sheet in the refrigerator for about 15-20 minutes, or until the chocolate coating has set.

Once the chocolate coating is firm, remove the chocolate-covered strawberries from the refrigerator and serve.

Enjoy your dairy-free chocolate-covered strawberries as a delicious and indulgent treat!

These dairy-free chocolate-covered strawberries are perfect for special occasions, parties, or simply as a sweet and healthy snack. They can also be stored in an airtight container in the refrigerator for a day or two, although they are best enjoyed fresh.

Vegan Chocolate Peanut Butter Cups

Ingredients:

- 1 cup dairy-free chocolate chips or chopped dairy-free chocolate bar
- 1/4 cup creamy peanut butter (make sure it's vegan)
- 2 tablespoons powdered sugar (optional, for sweetening the peanut butter)
- Pinch of salt (optional, to taste)
- Mini cupcake liners

Instructions:

Line a mini muffin tin with mini cupcake liners and set aside.

In a microwave-safe bowl or using a double boiler, melt the dairy-free chocolate chips or chopped dairy-free chocolate bar until smooth. If using a microwave, heat the chocolate in 30-second intervals, stirring between each interval until melted.

Spoon a small amount of melted chocolate into the bottom of each cupcake liner, spreading it evenly to cover the bottom. You want enough chocolate to form a solid base for the peanut butter filling. Reserve some melted chocolate for the top layer.

In a separate bowl, mix together the creamy peanut butter, powdered sugar (if using), and a pinch of salt (if desired) until smooth and well combined. Taste the peanut butter mixture and adjust the sweetness and saltiness according to your preference.

Spoon a small amount of the peanut butter mixture on top of the chocolate layer in each cupcake liner, spreading it out to cover the chocolate layer completely.

Once all the peanut butter filling has been added, spoon the remaining melted chocolate over the top of each peanut butter-filled cup, covering it completely and smoothing out the tops.

Optional: Sprinkle a pinch of sea salt or chopped peanuts on top of each chocolate peanut butter cup for added flavor and texture.

Place the muffin tin in the refrigerator for about 30 minutes, or until the chocolate peanut butter cups are firm and set.

Once set, remove the chocolate peanut butter cups from the muffin tin and peel away the cupcake liners.

Serve and enjoy your delicious vegan chocolate peanut butter cups!

These vegan chocolate peanut butter cups are perfect for satisfying your sweet cravings and are sure to be a hit with vegans and non-vegans alike. Store any leftovers in an airtight container in the refrigerator for up to a week.

Dairy-Free Chocolate Popsicles

Ingredients:

- 1 can (13.5 oz) full-fat coconut milk
- 1/4 cup cocoa powder
- 1/4 cup maple syrup or agave nectar (adjust to taste)
- 1 teaspoon vanilla extract
- Pinch of salt
- Optional: dairy-free chocolate chips, chopped nuts, or shredded coconut for added texture

Instructions:

In a blender, combine the full-fat coconut milk, cocoa powder, maple syrup or agave nectar, vanilla extract, and a pinch of salt. Blend until smooth and well combined.

Taste the mixture and adjust the sweetness if necessary by adding more maple syrup or agave nectar.

If you're using any optional add-ins like dairy-free chocolate chips, chopped nuts, or shredded coconut, stir them into the mixture.

Pour the chocolate mixture into popsicle molds, leaving a little space at the top for expansion. If you don't have popsicle molds, you can use small paper cups and popsicle sticks.

Insert popsicle sticks into the molds or cups. If your molds have covers, put them on.

Place the popsicle molds in the freezer and freeze for at least 4-6 hours, or until the popsicles are completely frozen.

Once the popsicles are frozen solid, remove them from the molds by running warm water over the outside of the molds for a few seconds. Gently wiggle the popsicles to release them from the molds.

Serve and enjoy your dairy-free chocolate popsicles immediately, or store them in an airtight container or freezer bag in the freezer for later.

These dairy-free chocolate popsicles are a refreshing and indulgent treat, perfect for hot summer days or anytime you're craving something sweet and chocolaty. Feel free to get creative with the recipe by adding different flavors or toppings to customize your popsicles!

Chocolate Covered Dates

Ingredients:

- Medjool dates, pitted
- Dairy-free chocolate chips or chopped dairy-free chocolate bar
- Optional toppings: chopped nuts, shredded coconut, sea salt

Instructions:

Line a baking sheet with parchment paper or wax paper and set it aside.
Remove the pits from the dates by making a small slit on one side and gently removing the pit. Ensure that the dates are not torn apart in the process.
In a microwave-safe bowl or using a double boiler, melt the dairy-free chocolate chips or chopped dairy-free chocolate bar until smooth. If using a microwave, heat the chocolate in 30-second intervals, stirring between each interval until melted.
Holding a pitted date by the stem, dip it into the melted chocolate, coating it halfway or entirely, as desired. Allow any excess chocolate to drip off.
Place the chocolate-covered date onto the prepared baking sheet.
If you're using any optional toppings such as chopped nuts, shredded coconut, or sea salt, sprinkle them onto the chocolate-covered dates while the chocolate is still melted.
Repeat the process with the remaining dates, dipping and topping them as desired.
Once all the dates are coated and topped, place the baking sheet in the refrigerator for about 15-20 minutes, or until the chocolate coating has set.
Once the chocolate coating is firm, remove the chocolate-covered dates from the refrigerator and serve.
Enjoy your delicious chocolate-covered dates as a sweet and indulgent treat!

These chocolate-covered dates are perfect for satisfying your sweet cravings and are sure to be a hit at any gathering or as a simple dessert. They can also be stored in an airtight container in the refrigerator for a few days, although they are best enjoyed fresh.

Vegan Chocolate Cheesecake

Ingredients:

For the crust:

- 1 1/2 cups vegan chocolate cookies or graham crackers, crushed
- 1/4 cup melted vegan butter or coconut oil

For the filling:

- 2 cups raw cashews, soaked in water overnight or for at least 4 hours
- 1/2 cup canned coconut cream (the solid part from a can of full-fat coconut milk)
- 1/2 cup maple syrup or agave nectar
- 1/4 cup cocoa powder
- 1/4 cup melted dairy-free chocolate chips or chopped dairy-free chocolate bar
- 2 tablespoons coconut oil, melted
- 2 teaspoons vanilla extract
- Pinch of salt

For the chocolate ganache topping (optional):

- 1/4 cup canned coconut cream
- 1/4 cup dairy-free chocolate chips or chopped dairy-free chocolate bar

Instructions:

Preheat your oven to 350°F (175°C). Grease a 9-inch springform pan and line the bottom with parchment paper.

In a food processor, pulse the vegan chocolate cookies or graham crackers until finely crushed. Add the melted vegan butter or coconut oil and pulse until well combined.

Press the crust mixture into the bottom of the prepared springform pan, using the back of a spoon or your fingers to press it down firmly. Bake the crust in the preheated oven for 10 minutes, then remove it from the oven and let it cool while you prepare the filling.

Drain the soaked cashews and rinse them thoroughly under cold water.

In a high-speed blender or food processor, combine the soaked cashews, canned coconut cream, maple syrup or agave nectar, cocoa powder, melted dairy-free chocolate, melted coconut oil, vanilla extract, and a pinch of salt. Blend until smooth and creamy, scraping down the sides of the blender or food processor as needed.

Pour the chocolate cheesecake filling over the cooled crust in the springform pan, smoothing it out evenly with a spatula.

Place the cheesecake in the refrigerator to set for at least 4 hours, or preferably overnight.

If making the chocolate ganache topping, heat the canned coconut cream in a small saucepan until it just begins to simmer. Remove from heat and add the dairy-free chocolate chips or chopped chocolate. Let it sit for a minute, then stir until smooth and glossy.

Pour the chocolate ganache over the chilled cheesecake, spreading it out evenly with a spatula. Return the cheesecake to the refrigerator to let the ganache set for about 30 minutes.

Once the ganache is set, carefully run a knife around the edge of the springform pan to loosen the cheesecake. Remove the sides of the pan.

Slice the vegan chocolate cheesecake and serve chilled. Enjoy this decadent dessert!

This vegan chocolate cheesecake is rich, creamy, and full of chocolate flavor, making it a perfect indulgence for special occasions or any time you're craving a delicious treat.

Dairy-Free Chocolate Coconut Milkshake

Ingredients:

- 1 can (13.5 oz) full-fat coconut milk, chilled
- 1/2 cup dairy-free chocolate chips or chopped dairy-free chocolate bar
- 2 tablespoons cocoa powder
- 2 tablespoons maple syrup or agave nectar (adjust to taste)
- 1/2 teaspoon vanilla extract
- Pinch of salt
- Ice cubes (optional, for a colder milkshake)
- Shredded coconut or dairy-free whipped cream for garnish (optional)

Instructions:

Chill the can of full-fat coconut milk in the refrigerator for at least a few hours or overnight. Chilling helps separate the cream from the liquid.

Once chilled, open the can of coconut milk and scoop out the thick coconut cream that has risen to the top, leaving behind the coconut water at the bottom. You should get about 1 cup of coconut cream.

In a small saucepan or microwave-safe bowl, heat the coconut cream until just simmering. Remove from heat and add the dairy-free chocolate chips or chopped chocolate. Let it sit for a minute, then stir until the chocolate is melted and the mixture is smooth and creamy.

In a blender, combine the melted chocolate coconut cream mixture, cocoa powder, maple syrup or agave nectar, vanilla extract, and a pinch of salt. If you like your milkshake colder, you can also add a handful of ice cubes at this point. Blend the mixture until smooth and creamy. Taste and adjust the sweetness if necessary by adding more maple syrup or agave nectar.

Pour the chocolate coconut milkshake into glasses and garnish with shredded coconut or dairy-free whipped cream if desired.

Serve immediately and enjoy your delicious dairy-free chocolate coconut milkshake!

This creamy and indulgent milkshake is perfect for satisfying your chocolate cravings while being dairy-free and vegan-friendly. It's a refreshing treat for any time of the year!

Chocolate Quinoa Breakfast Bowl

Ingredients:

- 1/2 cup quinoa, rinsed
- 1 cup canned coconut milk or almond milk
- 2 tablespoons cocoa powder
- 2 tablespoons maple syrup or honey (adjust to taste)
- 1/2 teaspoon vanilla extract
- Pinch of salt
- Optional toppings: sliced bananas, berries, chopped nuts, shredded coconut, chia seeds, or dairy-free yogurt

Instructions:

In a medium saucepan, combine the rinsed quinoa and coconut milk or almond milk. Bring to a boil over medium heat.

Once boiling, reduce the heat to low and cover the saucepan with a lid. Simmer for about 15-20 minutes, or until the quinoa is cooked and the liquid is absorbed. Stir occasionally to prevent sticking.

While the quinoa is cooking, in a small bowl, whisk together the cocoa powder, maple syrup or honey, vanilla extract, and a pinch of salt until smooth. Adjust the sweetness to your liking.

Once the quinoa is cooked, remove the saucepan from the heat and stir in the chocolate mixture until well combined.

Taste the chocolate quinoa and adjust the sweetness or cocoa flavor if desired. Divide the chocolate quinoa into serving bowls.

Top the chocolate quinoa with your favorite toppings such as sliced bananas, berries, chopped nuts, shredded coconut, chia seeds, or dairy-free yogurt.

Serve warm and enjoy your delicious and nutritious chocolate quinoa breakfast bowl!

This chocolate quinoa breakfast bowl is a satisfying and healthy way to start your day. It's packed with protein, fiber, and flavor, making it perfect for a nourishing breakfast that will keep you energized throughout the morning. Feel free to customize the toppings to your preference for added variety and enjoyment!

Dairy-Free Chocolate Protein Balls

Ingredients:

- 1 cup rolled oats
- 1/2 cup dairy-free chocolate protein powder
- 1/4 cup almond butter or peanut butter (make sure it's dairy-free)
- 1/4 cup maple syrup or agave nectar
- 2 tablespoons cocoa powder
- 1 teaspoon vanilla extract
- Pinch of salt
- Optional: dairy-free chocolate chips, shredded coconut, chopped nuts for coating

Instructions:

> In a food processor, combine the rolled oats, dairy-free chocolate protein powder, almond butter or peanut butter, maple syrup or agave nectar, cocoa powder, vanilla extract, and a pinch of salt. Pulse until the mixture comes together and forms a dough-like consistency.
> If the mixture seems too dry, you can add a little more almond butter or peanut butter, or a splash of water to help bind everything together.
> Once the mixture is well combined, scoop out tablespoon-sized portions and roll them into balls using your hands. If desired, you can press a few dairy-free chocolate chips, shredded coconut, or chopped nuts onto the surface of each ball for added texture and flavor.
> Place the chocolate protein balls on a baking sheet lined with parchment paper. Once all the mixture has been rolled into balls, place the baking sheet in the refrigerator for about 30 minutes to allow the protein balls to firm up.
> Once firm, remove the chocolate protein balls from the refrigerator and transfer them to an airtight container for storage.
> Enjoy your dairy-free chocolate protein balls as a satisfying and nutritious snack anytime you need a quick energy boost!

These chocolate protein balls are not only delicious but also packed with protein, fiber, and healthy fats, making them a great option for pre or post-workout snacks, midday pick-me-ups, or anytime you're craving something sweet and satisfying. Plus, they're easy to customize with your favorite mix-ins and coatings!

Vegan Chocolate Raspberry Tart

Ingredients:

For the crust:

- 1 1/2 cups almond flour
- 1/4 cup cocoa powder
- 1/4 cup maple syrup
- 2 tablespoons melted coconut oil
- Pinch of salt

For the filling:

- 1 cup canned coconut cream
- 1/2 cup dairy-free chocolate chips or chopped dairy-free chocolate bar
- 1 tablespoon maple syrup
- 1 teaspoon vanilla extract

For the raspberry topping:

- 1 cup fresh raspberries
- 1 tablespoon maple syrup
- 1 tablespoon water
- 1 teaspoon cornstarch

Instructions:

Preheat your oven to 350°F (175°C).
In a mixing bowl, combine almond flour, cocoa powder, maple syrup, melted coconut oil, and a pinch of salt. Mix until well combined and a dough forms. Press the dough into a 9-inch tart pan, making sure to press it evenly along the bottom and up the sides. Use a fork to prick the bottom of the crust.
Bake the crust in the preheated oven for about 10-12 minutes, or until it is set. Remove from the oven and let it cool completely.
In a small saucepan, heat the coconut cream over medium heat until it just begins to simmer. Remove from heat and add the dairy-free chocolate chips or chopped chocolate. Let it sit for a minute, then stir until smooth and creamy. Stir in maple syrup and vanilla extract.

Pour the chocolate filling into the cooled tart crust and spread it out evenly. Place the tart in the refrigerator to set for at least 1 hour.

While the tart is chilling, prepare the raspberry topping. In a small saucepan, combine fresh raspberries, maple syrup, water, and cornstarch. Cook over medium heat, stirring gently, until the raspberries break down and the mixture thickens slightly, about 5-7 minutes. Remove from heat and let it cool.

Once the chocolate filling is set, spread the raspberry topping over the top of the tart.

Return the tart to the refrigerator and let it chill for another 30 minutes to allow the raspberry topping to set.

Serve slices of the vegan chocolate raspberry tart chilled and enjoy!

This tart is rich, chocolatey, and bursting with fresh raspberry flavor. It's the perfect dessert for any occasion, and since it's vegan, it's suitable for those with dietary restrictions. Enjoy!

Dairy-Free Chocolate Cherry Smoothie

Ingredients:

- 1 cup frozen cherries, pitted
- 1 ripe banana, peeled and frozen
- 1 tablespoon cocoa powder
- 1 cup dairy-free milk (such as almond milk, coconut milk, or oat milk)
- 1 tablespoon maple syrup or agave nectar (optional, adjust to taste)
- 1/2 teaspoon vanilla extract
- Ice cubes (optional, for a thicker smoothie)

Instructions:

Place the frozen cherries, frozen banana, cocoa powder, dairy-free milk, maple syrup or agave nectar (if using), and vanilla extract in a blender.
If you prefer a thicker smoothie, you can add a handful of ice cubes to the blender.
Blend all the ingredients together until smooth and creamy. If the smoothie is too thick, you can add more dairy-free milk, a little at a time, until you reach your desired consistency.
Taste the smoothie and adjust the sweetness if necessary by adding more maple syrup or agave nectar.
Once the smoothie is blended to your liking, pour it into glasses and serve immediately.
Optionally, you can garnish the smoothie with a few fresh cherries or a sprinkle of cocoa powder before serving.
Enjoy your refreshing and indulgent Dairy-Free Chocolate Cherry Smoothie!

This smoothie is not only delicious but also packed with antioxidants from the cherries and nutrients from the banana. It's a perfect way to start your day or enjoy as a healthy snack or dessert. Feel free to customize the recipe by adding protein powder, chia seeds, or other fruits for extra nutrition and flavor.

Chocolate Banana Nice Cream

Ingredients:

- 3 ripe bananas, peeled, sliced, and frozen
- 2 tablespoons cocoa powder
- 1-2 tablespoons maple syrup or agave nectar (optional, adjust to taste)
- 1/2 teaspoon vanilla extract
- Optional toppings: sliced bananas, chopped nuts, dairy-free chocolate chips, shredded coconut

Instructions:

Slice the ripe bananas and place them in a single layer on a parchment-lined baking sheet. Freeze the banana slices for at least 2-3 hours or until completely frozen.
Once the banana slices are frozen, transfer them to a food processor or high-speed blender.
Add the cocoa powder, maple syrup or agave nectar (if using), and vanilla extract to the frozen banana slices.
Blend the mixture on high speed until smooth and creamy, scraping down the sides of the food processor or blender as needed. You may need to stop and stir the mixture a few times to ensure even blending.
Taste the nice cream and adjust the sweetness or cocoa flavor if necessary by adding more maple syrup or cocoa powder.
Once the nice cream reaches your desired consistency and flavor, transfer it to a container and freeze for about 30 minutes to firm up slightly.
Serve the chocolate banana nice cream in bowls or cones and top with your favorite toppings such as sliced bananas, chopped nuts, dairy-free chocolate chips, or shredded coconut.
Enjoy your delicious and guilt-free Chocolate Banana Nice Cream!

This creamy and decadent treat is perfect for satisfying your sweet cravings while being naturally sweetened and packed with nutrients from the bananas. It's a great dessert option for those following a dairy-free or vegan diet or anyone looking for a healthier alternative to traditional ice cream.

Vegan Chocolate Granola Bars

Ingredients:

- 2 cups rolled oats
- 1/2 cup chopped nuts (such as almonds, walnuts, or pecans)
- 1/4 cup seeds (such as pumpkin seeds or sunflower seeds)
- 1/4 cup shredded coconut
- 1/4 cup dairy-free chocolate chips
- 1/4 cup dried fruit (such as raisins, cranberries, or chopped dates)
- 1/4 cup maple syrup or agave nectar
- 1/4 cup melted coconut oil or almond butter
- 1/4 cup cocoa powder
- 1 teaspoon vanilla extract
- Pinch of salt

Instructions:

Preheat your oven to 350°F (175°C). Line an 8x8 inch baking pan with parchment paper, leaving some overhang on the sides for easy removal later.

In a large mixing bowl, combine the rolled oats, chopped nuts, seeds, shredded coconut, dairy-free chocolate chips, and dried fruit. Stir to combine.

In a separate small bowl, whisk together the maple syrup or agave nectar, melted coconut oil or almond butter, cocoa powder, vanilla extract, and a pinch of salt until smooth and well combined.

Pour the wet ingredients over the dry ingredients in the large mixing bowl. Stir until all the dry ingredients are evenly coated with the chocolate mixture.

Transfer the mixture into the prepared baking pan. Use a spatula or the back of a spoon to press the mixture firmly and evenly into the pan.

Bake in the preheated oven for 20-25 minutes, or until the edges are golden brown and the top is set.

Remove the pan from the oven and let the granola bars cool completely in the pan on a wire rack.

Once cooled, use the parchment paper overhang to lift the granola slab out of the pan. Place it on a cutting board and use a sharp knife to cut it into bars or squares.

Store the vegan chocolate granola bars in an airtight container at room temperature for up to a week, or in the refrigerator for longer shelf life.

Enjoy your homemade vegan chocolate granola bars as a tasty and nutritious snack on the go or as a sweet treat any time of the day!

These vegan chocolate granola bars are customizable, so feel free to experiment with different nuts, seeds, dried fruits, or additional add-ins like coconut flakes or spices to suit your taste preferences.

Dairy-Free Chocolate Oatmeal Cookies

Ingredients:

- 1 cup rolled oats
- 1 cup all-purpose flour
- 1/2 cup cocoa powder
- 1 teaspoon baking powder
- 1/2 teaspoon baking soda
- 1/4 teaspoon salt
- 1/2 cup coconut oil, melted
- 1/2 cup maple syrup or agave nectar
- 1/4 cup brown sugar
- 1 flax egg (1 tablespoon ground flaxseed mixed with 3 tablespoons water)
- 1 teaspoon vanilla extract
- 1/2 cup dairy-free chocolate chips

Instructions:

Preheat your oven to 350°F (175°C). Line a baking sheet with parchment paper or silicone baking mat.
In a large mixing bowl, combine the rolled oats, all-purpose flour, cocoa powder, baking powder, baking soda, and salt. Stir until well combined.
In a separate bowl, whisk together the melted coconut oil, maple syrup or agave nectar, brown sugar, flax egg, and vanilla extract until smooth.
Pour the wet ingredients into the dry ingredients and mix until a dough forms.
Fold in the dairy-free chocolate chips until evenly distributed.
Scoop tablespoon-sized portions of dough and roll them into balls. Place them on the prepared baking sheet, leaving some space between each cookie.
Flatten each cookie slightly with the palm of your hand or the back of a spoon.
Bake in the preheated oven for 10-12 minutes, or until the edges are set. The cookies may still seem slightly soft in the center, but they will firm up as they cool.
Remove the baking sheet from the oven and let the cookies cool on the pan for a few minutes before transferring them to a wire rack to cool completely.
Once cooled, enjoy your dairy-free chocolate oatmeal cookies with a glass of dairy-free milk or your favorite hot beverage!

These cookies are soft, chewy, and full of chocolate flavor, making them a perfect treat for any occasion. They're also customizable, so feel free to add chopped nuts, dried fruits, or shredded coconut for extra texture and flavor. Enjoy!

Chocolate Coconut Bliss Balls

Ingredients:

- 1 cup Medjool dates, pitted
- 1 cup shredded coconut, unsweetened
- 1/4 cup cocoa powder
- 1/4 cup almond flour or ground almonds
- 1 teaspoon vanilla extract
- Pinch of salt
- 2-3 tablespoons water (if needed)

Optional coatings:

- Additional shredded coconut
- Cocoa powder
- Crushed nuts

Instructions:

Place the pitted dates in a food processor and pulse until they form a sticky paste.

Add shredded coconut, cocoa powder, almond flour, vanilla extract, and a pinch of salt to the food processor with the date paste.

Process the mixture until well combined and it forms a thick, sticky dough. If the mixture seems too dry, add 1-2 tablespoons of water and process again until the desired consistency is reached.

Once the mixture is ready, scoop out small portions and roll them into balls using your hands. If desired, you can roll the balls in additional shredded coconut, cocoa powder, or crushed nuts for extra flavor and texture.

Place the rolled bliss balls on a baking sheet lined with parchment paper and refrigerate them for at least 30 minutes to firm up.

Once chilled, the chocolate coconut bliss balls are ready to enjoy! Store any leftovers in an airtight container in the refrigerator for up to a week.

These chocolate coconut bliss balls are a perfect energy-boosting snack or dessert.

They're naturally sweetened, packed with fiber, and loaded with coconut and chocolate flavor. Plus, they're vegan, gluten-free, and dairy-free, making them suitable for various dietary preferences. Enjoy!

Vegan Chocolate Espresso Cake

Ingredients:

For the cake:

- 1 1/2 cups all-purpose flour
- 1 cup granulated sugar
- 1/3 cup cocoa powder
- 1 teaspoon baking soda
- 1/2 teaspoon salt
- 1 cup brewed espresso or strong coffee, cooled
- 1/2 cup vegetable oil
- 2 tablespoons apple cider vinegar
- 1 teaspoon vanilla extract

For the frosting:

- 1 cup dairy-free dark chocolate chips or chopped dairy-free chocolate bar
- 1/2 cup canned coconut milk (the solid part from a can of full-fat coconut milk)
- 2 tablespoons brewed espresso or strong coffee, cooled
- 1 tablespoon maple syrup or agave nectar

Optional garnish:

- Vegan chocolate shavings
- Cocoa powder
- Fresh berries

Instructions:

Preheat your oven to 350°F (175°C). Grease and flour an 8-inch round cake pan or line it with parchment paper.
In a large mixing bowl, whisk together the all-purpose flour, granulated sugar, cocoa powder, baking soda, and salt until well combined.
In a separate bowl, whisk together the brewed espresso or coffee, vegetable oil, apple cider vinegar, and vanilla extract until smooth.
Pour the wet ingredients into the dry ingredients and mix until just combined. Be careful not to overmix.
Pour the batter into the prepared cake pan and spread it out evenly.

Bake in the preheated oven for 25-30 minutes, or until a toothpick inserted into the center comes out clean.

Remove the cake from the oven and let it cool in the pan for about 10 minutes. Then, transfer it to a wire rack to cool completely.

While the cake is cooling, prepare the frosting. In a small saucepan, heat the canned coconut milk over medium heat until it just begins to simmer. Remove from heat and add the dairy-free dark chocolate chips or chopped chocolate. Let it sit for a minute, then stir until smooth and creamy. Stir in the brewed espresso or coffee and maple syrup or agave nectar.

Let the frosting cool for a few minutes until it thickens slightly.

Once the cake has cooled completely, spread the frosting evenly over the top of the cake.

Optionally, garnish the cake with vegan chocolate shavings, cocoa powder, or fresh berries.

Slice and serve your delicious Vegan Chocolate Espresso Cake!

This cake is rich, moist, and full of chocolate and espresso flavor. It's perfect for special occasions or anytime you're craving a decadent dessert. Enjoy!

Dairy-Free Chocolate Avocado Smoothie Bowl

Ingredients:

For the smoothie bowl:

- 1 ripe avocado, peeled and pitted
- 1 large ripe banana, peeled and frozen
- 2 tablespoons cocoa powder
- 1 cup dairy-free milk (such as almond milk, coconut milk, or oat milk)
- 1 tablespoon maple syrup or agave nectar (optional, adjust to taste)
- 1/2 teaspoon vanilla extract
- Pinch of salt
- Ice cubes (optional, for a thicker consistency)

For toppings (optional):

- Sliced banana
- Berries (such as strawberries, raspberries, or blueberries)
- Granola
- Chia seeds
- Shredded coconut
- Nuts or seeds (such as almonds, walnuts, or pumpkin seeds)
- Dairy-free chocolate chips

Instructions:

In a blender, combine the ripe avocado, frozen banana, cocoa powder, dairy-free milk, maple syrup or agave nectar (if using), vanilla extract, and a pinch of salt. If you prefer a thicker smoothie bowl, you can add a handful of ice cubes to the blender.
Blend the ingredients on high speed until smooth and creamy. If necessary, stop and scrape down the sides of the blender to ensure all ingredients are well incorporated.
Taste the smoothie and adjust the sweetness or cocoa flavor if necessary by adding more maple syrup or cocoa powder.
Once the smoothie reaches your desired consistency and flavor, pour it into a bowl.

Add your favorite toppings to the smoothie bowl, such as sliced banana, berries, granola, chia seeds, shredded coconut, nuts or seeds, and dairy-free chocolate chips.

Serve your Dairy-Free Chocolate Avocado Smoothie Bowl immediately and enjoy!

This smoothie bowl is not only delicious but also packed with healthy fats from the avocado, potassium from the banana, and antioxidants from the cocoa powder. It's a satisfying and nutritious breakfast or snack option that's sure to satisfy your chocolate cravings. Feel free to customize the toppings according to your preferences and enjoy this indulgent treat!

Chocolate Hazelnut Energy Bites

Ingredients:

- 1 cup pitted dates
- 1 cup roasted hazelnuts
- 2 tablespoons cocoa powder
- 1 tablespoon maple syrup or agave nectar (optional, for added sweetness)
- 1/2 teaspoon vanilla extract
- Pinch of salt
- 2-3 tablespoons water (if needed)

Optional coatings:

- Finely chopped hazelnuts
- Shredded coconut
- Cocoa powder

Instructions:

Place the pitted dates in a food processor and pulse until they are broken down into small pieces.

Add the roasted hazelnuts, cocoa powder, maple syrup or agave nectar (if using), vanilla extract, and a pinch of salt to the food processor.

Process the mixture until it starts to come together into a sticky dough. If the mixture seems too dry, add 2-3 tablespoons of water, one tablespoon at a time, and continue processing until the mixture forms a thick, sticky dough.

Once the mixture is ready, scoop out tablespoon-sized portions and roll them into balls using your hands.

Roll the balls in optional coatings such as finely chopped hazelnuts, shredded coconut, or cocoa powder, pressing gently to adhere the coatings to the surface of the balls.

Place the chocolate hazelnut energy bites on a baking sheet lined with parchment paper and refrigerate them for at least 30 minutes to firm up.

Once chilled, the energy bites are ready to enjoy! Store any leftovers in an airtight container in the refrigerator for up to a week.

These Chocolate Hazelnut Energy Bites are perfect for a quick and satisfying snack on the go. They're naturally sweetened, packed with protein and fiber, and loaded with the rich flavors of chocolate and hazelnut. Enjoy!

Vegan Chocolate Chia Pudding Parfait

Ingredients:

For the chocolate chia pudding:

- 1/4 cup chia seeds
- 1 cup canned coconut milk or almond milk
- 2 tablespoons cocoa powder
- 2 tablespoons maple syrup or agave nectar
- 1/2 teaspoon vanilla extract
- Pinch of salt

For assembling the parfait:

- Vegan granola or crushed nuts
- Fresh berries or sliced fruits
- Dairy-free yogurt or coconut whipped cream (optional)

Instructions:

In a mixing bowl, whisk together the chia seeds, canned coconut milk or almond milk, cocoa powder, maple syrup or agave nectar, vanilla extract, and a pinch of salt until well combined.
Let the mixture sit for about 5 minutes, then whisk again to prevent clumps from forming. Repeat this process a couple more times over the next 15 minutes.
Cover the bowl and refrigerate the chocolate chia pudding mixture for at least 2 hours, or preferably overnight, to allow it to thicken.
Once the chia pudding has thickened, give it a good stir to ensure a smooth consistency.
To assemble the parfait, layer the chocolate chia pudding with vegan granola or crushed nuts and fresh berries or sliced fruits in serving glasses or jars.
Optionally, you can add a layer of dairy-free yogurt or coconut whipped cream between the layers for extra creaminess.
Repeat the layers until the glasses or jars are filled to your liking.
Garnish the top of each parfait with additional berries, nuts, or a drizzle of maple syrup, if desired.
Serve the vegan chocolate chia pudding parfaits immediately, or refrigerate them until ready to serve.

These Vegan Chocolate Chia Pudding Parfaits are a delightful treat that's both satisfying and healthy. They're packed with fiber, omega-3 fatty acids, and antioxidants, making them a perfect guilt-free indulgence for any time of day. Enjoy!

Dairy-Free Chocolate Peppermint Patties

Ingredients:

For the peppermint filling:

- 1/2 cup coconut butter (not coconut oil), softened
- 1/4 cup maple syrup or agave nectar
- 1/2 teaspoon peppermint extract
- Pinch of salt

For the chocolate coating:

- 1 cup dairy-free chocolate chips or chopped dairy-free chocolate bar
- 1 tablespoon coconut oil

Instructions:

In a mixing bowl, combine the softened coconut butter, maple syrup or agave nectar, peppermint extract, and a pinch of salt. Mix until well combined and smooth.

Place the bowl in the refrigerator for about 15-20 minutes to firm up the peppermint filling slightly.

Once the filling has firmed up a bit, scoop out small portions of the mixture and roll them into balls using your hands. Place the balls on a parchment-lined baking sheet.

Flatten each ball slightly with your fingers or the back of a spoon to form patties. Place the baking sheet in the freezer for about 30 minutes to firm up the patties further.

In the meantime, prepare the chocolate coating. In a microwave-safe bowl or using a double boiler, melt the dairy-free chocolate chips or chopped chocolate bar with the coconut oil until smooth and well combined.

Remove the peppermint patties from the freezer. Using a fork or dipping tools, dip each patty into the melted chocolate mixture, making sure it's fully coated.

Tap off any excess chocolate and place the coated patties back on the parchment-lined baking sheet.

Once all the patties are coated, return the baking sheet to the freezer for about 10-15 minutes, or until the chocolate coating is set.

Once set, remove the peppermint patties from the freezer and transfer them to an airtight container. Store them in the refrigerator until ready to serve.

Enjoy your homemade Dairy-Free Chocolate Peppermint Patties as a delicious and refreshing treat!

These chocolate peppermint patties are perfect for the holidays or any time you're craving a sweet and minty indulgence. They're vegan, dairy-free, and free of refined sugars, making them a healthier alternative to store-bought candy. Enjoy!

Chocolate Almond Butter Energy Bars

Ingredients:

- 1 cup rolled oats
- 1/2 cup almond butter
- 1/4 cup maple syrup or honey
- 1/4 cup chopped almonds
- 1/4 cup dairy-free chocolate chips
- 2 tablespoons cocoa powder
- 1 tablespoon chia seeds (optional)
- 1 teaspoon vanilla extract
- Pinch of salt

Instructions:

Preheat your oven to 350°F (175°C). Line an 8x8 inch baking pan with parchment paper, leaving some overhang on the sides for easy removal later.

Spread the rolled oats evenly on a baking sheet and toast them in the preheated oven for about 5-7 minutes, or until lightly golden and fragrant. Remove from the oven and let them cool.

In a large mixing bowl, combine the toasted oats, almond butter, maple syrup or honey, chopped almonds, dairy-free chocolate chips, cocoa powder, chia seeds (if using), vanilla extract, and a pinch of salt. Mix until all the ingredients are well combined and form a sticky dough.

Transfer the dough into the prepared baking pan and press it down firmly and evenly using the back of a spoon or your hands.

Place the baking pan in the refrigerator for at least 1-2 hours, or until the mixture is firm and set.

Once the mixture is firm, remove the baking pan from the refrigerator and use the parchment paper overhang to lift the energy bars out of the pan. Place them on a cutting board.

Use a sharp knife to cut the chilled mixture into bars or squares of your desired size.

Store the Chocolate Almond Butter Energy Bars in an airtight container in the refrigerator for up to a week.

These energy bars are perfect for a quick and nutritious snack on the go. They're packed with fiber, protein, and healthy fats from the almonds and almond butter, making them a satisfying and energizing treat. Enjoy!

Vegan Chocolate Pumpkin Bread

Ingredients:

- 1 1/2 cups all-purpose flour
- 1/2 cup cocoa powder
- 1 teaspoon baking soda
- 1/2 teaspoon baking powder
- 1/4 teaspoon salt
- 1 teaspoon ground cinnamon
- 1/2 teaspoon ground nutmeg
- 1/4 teaspoon ground cloves
- 1 cup pumpkin puree
- 1/2 cup maple syrup or agave nectar
- 1/4 cup coconut oil, melted
- 1/4 cup almond milk or any other dairy-free milk
- 1 teaspoon vanilla extract
- 1/2 cup dairy-free chocolate chips (optional)

Instructions:

Preheat your oven to 350°F (175°C). Grease a 9x5 inch loaf pan or line it with parchment paper.
In a large mixing bowl, whisk together the all-purpose flour, cocoa powder, baking soda, baking powder, salt, cinnamon, nutmeg, and cloves until well combined.
In another mixing bowl, combine the pumpkin puree, maple syrup or agave nectar, melted coconut oil, almond milk, and vanilla extract. Mix until smooth and well combined.
Pour the wet ingredients into the dry ingredients and mix until just combined. Be careful not to overmix.
If using, fold in the dairy-free chocolate chips until evenly distributed throughout the batter.
Pour the batter into the prepared loaf pan and spread it out evenly.
Bake in the preheated oven for 50-60 minutes, or until a toothpick inserted into the center comes out clean.
Remove the bread from the oven and let it cool in the pan for about 10 minutes. Then, transfer it to a wire rack to cool completely before slicing.
Once cooled, slice the Vegan Chocolate Pumpkin Bread and serve. Enjoy!

This Vegan Chocolate Pumpkin Bread is moist, flavorful, and perfect for enjoying during the fall season or any time of the year. It's a delicious and healthier alternative to traditional pumpkin bread, and it's sure to be a hit with vegans and non-vegans alike!

Dairy-Free Chocolate Coconut Ice Cream

Ingredients:

- 2 cans (13.5 oz each) full-fat coconut milk
- 1/2 cup cocoa powder
- 1/2 cup maple syrup or agave nectar (adjust to taste)
- 1 teaspoon vanilla extract
- Pinch of salt
- Optional add-ins: dairy-free chocolate chips, shredded coconut, chopped nuts

Instructions:

Make sure to chill the cans of coconut milk in the refrigerator for at least 8 hours or overnight. This will help separate the cream from the liquid.

Once chilled, carefully open the cans of coconut milk without shaking them. Scoop out the thick coconut cream that has risen to the top and place it in a mixing bowl, leaving behind the coconut water at the bottom. You should get about 1 1/2 to 2 cups of coconut cream.

Add cocoa powder, maple syrup or agave nectar, vanilla extract, and a pinch of salt to the coconut cream.

Using a hand mixer or a stand mixer with the whisk attachment, beat the mixture until smooth and well combined. Taste and adjust the sweetness if needed by adding more maple syrup or agave nectar.

If desired, fold in optional add-ins such as dairy-free chocolate chips, shredded coconut, or chopped nuts.

Transfer the mixture to an ice cream maker and churn according to the manufacturer's instructions until it reaches a soft-serve consistency.

If you don't have an ice cream maker, you can pour the mixture into a shallow dish and freeze it. Every 30 minutes, take it out of the freezer and stir vigorously to break up any ice crystals. Repeat this process until the ice cream is firm and creamy.

Once the ice cream is ready, transfer it to a freezer-safe container and freeze for at least 4 hours or until firm.

Before serving, let the ice cream sit at room temperature for a few minutes to soften slightly. Then scoop and enjoy your Dairy-Free Chocolate Coconut Ice Cream!

This dairy-free chocolate coconut ice cream is creamy, rich, and indulgent, with a delicious coconut flavor and a hint of chocolate. It's perfect for satisfying your sweet cravings on hot summer days or any time you're in the mood for a cool treat. Enjoy!

Chocolate Almond Milkshake

Ingredients:

- 2 cups chocolate almond milk (store-bought or homemade)
- 2 large scoops of dairy-free chocolate ice cream
- 2 tablespoons almond butter
- 1 tablespoon cocoa powder
- 1-2 tablespoons maple syrup or agave nectar (optional, adjust to taste)
- 1 teaspoon vanilla extract
- Ice cubes (optional, for a colder milkshake)
- Dairy-free whipped cream (optional, for garnish)
- Chocolate shavings or cocoa powder (optional, for garnish)

Instructions:

In a blender, combine the chocolate almond milk, dairy-free chocolate ice cream, almond butter, cocoa powder, maple syrup or agave nectar (if using), and vanilla extract.

If you prefer a colder milkshake, you can also add a handful of ice cubes to the blender.

Blend the mixture until smooth and creamy. Taste and adjust the sweetness if necessary by adding more maple syrup or agave nectar.

Once the milkshake reaches your desired consistency and sweetness, pour it into glasses.

Optionally, top the chocolate almond milkshake with dairy-free whipped cream and garnish with chocolate shavings or a sprinkle of cocoa powder.

Serve immediately and enjoy your delicious and refreshing Chocolate Almond Milkshake!

This creamy and indulgent milkshake is perfect for satisfying your chocolate cravings while being dairy-free and vegan-friendly. It's a refreshing treat for any time of the year!

Feel free to customize the recipe by adding a banana for extra creaminess or a handful of almonds for added texture and flavor. Enjoy!

Vegan Chocolate Coconut Flour Pancakes

Ingredients:

- 1/2 cup coconut flour
- 1/4 cup cocoa powder
- 2 tablespoons granulated sugar or coconut sugar
- 1 teaspoon baking powder
- Pinch of salt
- 1 cup dairy-free milk (such as almond milk, coconut milk, or soy milk)
- 2 tablespoons melted coconut oil or vegetable oil
- 1 teaspoon vanilla extract
- Dairy-free chocolate chips (optional, for extra chocolate flavor)
- Coconut oil or cooking spray, for greasing the pan

Instructions:

In a large mixing bowl, whisk together the coconut flour, cocoa powder, sugar, baking powder, and salt until well combined.

In a separate bowl, whisk together the dairy-free milk, melted coconut oil or vegetable oil, and vanilla extract.

Pour the wet ingredients into the dry ingredients and stir until just combined. Be careful not to overmix. If the batter seems too thick, you can add a little more dairy-free milk, a tablespoon at a time, until you reach your desired consistency.

If using, fold in dairy-free chocolate chips for extra chocolate flavor.

Let the batter sit for a few minutes to allow the coconut flour to absorb the liquid.

Heat a non-stick skillet or griddle over medium heat and lightly grease it with coconut oil or cooking spray.

Pour about 1/4 cup of batter onto the skillet for each pancake. Use the back of a spoon to spread the batter into a round shape.

Cook the pancakes for 2-3 minutes, or until bubbles form on the surface and the edges look set.

Carefully flip the pancakes and cook for an additional 1-2 minutes, or until cooked through and lightly browned on the bottom.

Transfer the cooked pancakes to a plate and keep them warm while you cook the remaining batter.

Serve the Vegan Chocolate Coconut Flour Pancakes warm with your favorite toppings such as maple syrup, fresh berries, sliced bananas, or dairy-free whipped cream.

These Vegan Chocolate Coconut Flour Pancakes are fluffy, chocolatey, and deliciously satisfying. They're perfect for a special breakfast or brunch and are sure to be a hit with vegans and non-vegans alike! Enjoy!

Dairy-Free Chocolate Raspberry Popsicles

Ingredients:

- 1 cup fresh raspberries
- 1 can (13.5 oz) coconut milk (full-fat)
- 1/4 cup cocoa powder
- 1/4 cup maple syrup or agave syrup
- 1 teaspoon vanilla extract
- Pinch of salt
- Popsicle molds

Instructions:

In a blender, combine the fresh raspberries, coconut milk, cocoa powder, maple syrup or agave syrup, vanilla extract, and a pinch of salt. Blend until smooth and well combined.

Taste the mixture and adjust sweetness if needed by adding more maple syrup/agave syrup.

Pour the mixture into popsicle molds, leaving a little space at the top for expansion. Insert popsicle sticks into the molds.

Place the popsicle molds in the freezer and freeze for at least 4-6 hours, or until the popsicles are completely frozen.

Once frozen, remove the popsicles from the molds by running warm water over the outside of the molds for a few seconds. Gently pull on the popsicle sticks to release the popsicles.

Serve immediately or store the popsicles in an airtight container or plastic bag in the freezer for later enjoyment.

These dairy-free chocolate raspberry popsicles are perfect for a refreshing and indulgent treat! Enjoy!

Chocolate Peanut Butter Rice Krispie Treats

Ingredients:

- 4 cups Rice Krispies cereal
- 1 cup smooth peanut butter
- 1 cup semi-sweet chocolate chips
- 1/2 cup maple syrup or honey
- 1/4 cup coconut oil
- 1 teaspoon vanilla extract
- Pinch of salt

Instructions:

Line a 9x9-inch baking dish with parchment paper or lightly grease it with oil. Set aside.
In a large mixing bowl, add the Rice Krispies cereal. Set aside.
In a microwave-safe bowl or a small saucepan over low heat, combine the peanut butter, chocolate chips, maple syrup or honey, coconut oil, vanilla extract, and a pinch of salt.
If using a microwave, heat the mixture in 30-second intervals, stirring in between, until everything is melted and well combined. If using a saucepan, stir constantly over low heat until everything is melted and smooth.
Once the peanut butter chocolate mixture is smooth, pour it over the Rice Krispies cereal in the mixing bowl. Use a spatula to gently fold and stir until the cereal is evenly coated with the chocolate peanut butter mixture.
Transfer the mixture into the prepared baking dish. Use the back of a spatula or your hands to press it evenly into the dish.
Place the dish in the refrigerator for at least 1 hour, or until the treats are firm and set.
Once set, remove the treats from the refrigerator and use a sharp knife to cut them into squares.
Serve and enjoy these delicious chocolate peanut butter Rice Krispie treats! Store any leftovers in an airtight container at room temperature or in the refrigerator for up to one week.

These treats are perfect for satisfying your chocolate and peanut butter cravings!

Vegan Chocolate Caramel Slice

Ingredients:

For the base:

- 1 1/2 cups (150g) almond flour
- 1/2 cup (50g) unsweetened shredded coconut
- 1/4 cup (60ml) maple syrup
- 3 tablespoons (45ml) coconut oil, melted
- Pinch of salt

For the caramel layer:

- 1 cup (240ml) coconut cream
- 1/2 cup (120ml) maple syrup
- 1/4 cup (60ml) coconut oil
- 1 teaspoon vanilla extract
- Pinch of salt

For the chocolate layer:

- 1 cup (180g) dairy-free dark chocolate chips or chopped chocolate
- 2 tablespoons (30ml) coconut oil

Instructions:

Preheat your oven to 350°F (175°C). Line an 8x8-inch baking dish with parchment paper, leaving some overhang for easy removal.

In a mixing bowl, combine almond flour, shredded coconut, maple syrup, melted coconut oil, and a pinch of salt. Mix until well combined and press the mixture firmly into the bottom of the prepared baking dish.

Bake the base in the preheated oven for 10-12 minutes, or until lightly golden brown. Remove from the oven and let it cool completely.

In a saucepan, combine coconut cream, maple syrup, coconut oil, vanilla extract, and a pinch of salt for the caramel layer. Bring the mixture to a simmer over medium heat, stirring constantly. Let it simmer for 5-7 minutes until it thickens slightly. Remove from heat and let it cool for a few minutes.

Pour the caramel mixture over the cooled base and spread it evenly. Place the baking dish in the refrigerator for about 1-2 hours, or until the caramel layer is firm.

Once the caramel layer is set, prepare the chocolate layer. In a microwave-safe bowl or over a double boiler, melt the dairy-free chocolate chips or chopped chocolate with coconut oil until smooth.

Pour the melted chocolate mixture over the caramel layer and spread it evenly. Return the baking dish to the refrigerator and chill for another 1-2 hours, or until the chocolate layer is set.

Once set, remove the chocolate caramel slice from the baking dish using the parchment paper overhang. Use a sharp knife to cut it into squares or bars.

Serve and enjoy your vegan chocolate caramel slice! Store any leftovers in an airtight container in the refrigerator for up to one week.

This indulgent treat is perfect for satisfying your sweet cravings while being dairy-free and vegan-friendly!

Dairy-Free Chocolate Macaroons

Ingredients:

- 2 cups shredded unsweetened coconut
- 1/2 cup cocoa powder
- 1/2 cup granulated sugar
- 2 tablespoons coconut oil, melted
- 2 tablespoons almond milk (or any other non-dairy milk)
- 1 teaspoon vanilla extract
- Pinch of salt

Instructions:

Preheat your oven to 350°F (175°C). Line a baking sheet with parchment paper.
In a large mixing bowl, combine the shredded coconut, cocoa powder, granulated sugar, melted coconut oil, almond milk, vanilla extract, and a pinch of salt. Mix until well combined.
Use a cookie scoop or your hands to scoop out about 1 tablespoon of the mixture and roll it into a ball. Place the ball onto the prepared baking sheet.
Repeat with the remaining mixture, spacing the balls about 1 inch apart.
Using your fingers or the back of a spoon, flatten each ball slightly to form a disc shape.
Bake the macaroons in the preheated oven for 10-12 minutes, or until the edges are slightly golden.
Remove the macaroons from the oven and let them cool on the baking sheet for a few minutes before transferring them to a wire rack to cool completely.
Once cooled, store the chocolate macaroons in an airtight container at room temperature for up to one week.

Enjoy your dairy-free chocolate macaroons as a delicious treat or dessert!

Chocolate Cherry Smoothie Bowl

Ingredients:

For the smoothie:

- 1 cup frozen cherries, pitted
- 1 ripe banana, peeled and frozen
- 1 tablespoon cocoa powder
- 1/2 cup almond milk (or any other plant-based milk)
- 1 tablespoon almond butter (or any other nut or seed butter)
- 1 tablespoon maple syrup or honey (optional, depending on sweetness preference)
- 1/2 teaspoon vanilla extract
- Pinch of salt

For toppings (optional):

- Fresh cherries, pitted and halved
- Chocolate chips
- Sliced almonds
- Shredded coconut
- Granola

Instructions:

In a blender, combine the frozen cherries, frozen banana, cocoa powder, almond milk, almond butter, maple syrup or honey (if using), vanilla extract, and a pinch of salt.

Blend the ingredients until smooth and creamy. If the mixture is too thick, you can add more almond milk, a tablespoon at a time, until you reach your desired consistency.

Once the smoothie is ready, pour it into a bowl.

Arrange your desired toppings on top of the smoothie bowl. You can use fresh cherries, chocolate chips, sliced almonds, shredded coconut, granola, or any other toppings you prefer.

Serve immediately and enjoy your delicious Chocolate Cherry Smoothie Bowl with a spoon!

This smoothie bowl is not only tasty but also packed with antioxidants from the cherries and nutrients from the other ingredients. It's perfect for a refreshing breakfast or a healthy snack any time of the day.

Vegan Chocolate Zucchini Muffins

Ingredients:

- 1 cup shredded zucchini (about 1 medium zucchini)
- 1 1/2 cups all-purpose flour
- 1/2 cup cocoa powder
- 1 teaspoon baking powder
- 1/2 teaspoon baking soda
- 1/4 teaspoon salt
- 1/2 cup granulated sugar
- 1/4 cup maple syrup or agave syrup
- 1/4 cup melted coconut oil or vegetable oil
- 1/2 cup non-dairy milk (such as almond milk, soy milk, or coconut milk)
- 1 teaspoon vanilla extract
- 1/2 cup dairy-free chocolate chips (optional)

Instructions:

Preheat your oven to 350°F (175°C). Line a muffin tin with paper liners or lightly grease the cups with oil.

Using a grater, shred the zucchini. Place the shredded zucchini in a clean kitchen towel or paper towels and squeeze out excess moisture.

In a large mixing bowl, sift together the all-purpose flour, cocoa powder, baking powder, baking soda, and salt.

In another mixing bowl, whisk together the granulated sugar, maple syrup or agave syrup, melted coconut oil or vegetable oil, non-dairy milk, and vanilla extract until well combined.

Add the wet ingredients to the dry ingredients and mix until just combined. Be careful not to overmix.

Gently fold in the shredded zucchini and chocolate chips (if using) into the batter.

Spoon the batter into the prepared muffin tin, filling each cup about 2/3 full.

Bake in the preheated oven for 18-20 minutes, or until a toothpick inserted into the center of a muffin comes out clean.

Remove the muffins from the oven and let them cool in the muffin tin for a few minutes before transferring them to a wire rack to cool completely.

Once cooled, store the vegan chocolate zucchini muffins in an airtight container at room temperature for up to 3 days, or in the refrigerator for up to 1 week.

Enjoy these moist and delicious vegan chocolate zucchini muffins as a tasty breakfast or snack!

Dairy-Free Chocolate Almond Milk Pudding

Ingredients:

- 2 cups unsweetened almond milk
- 1/4 cup cocoa powder
- 1/4 cup cornstarch
- 1/4 cup maple syrup or other sweetener of your choice
- 1 teaspoon vanilla extract
- Pinch of salt
- Dairy-free chocolate chips (optional, for garnish)
- Sliced almonds (optional, for garnish)

Instructions:

In a small bowl, whisk together the cocoa powder and cornstarch until well combined.
In a saucepan, heat the almond milk over medium heat until it starts to simmer. Be careful not to boil.
Once the almond milk is simmering, reduce the heat to low and gradually whisk in the cocoa powder and cornstarch mixture until smooth.
Cook the mixture over low heat, stirring constantly, until it thickens, about 5-7 minutes.
Once the pudding has thickened, remove it from the heat and stir in the maple syrup, vanilla extract, and a pinch of salt.
Transfer the pudding to serving bowls or glasses.
If desired, garnish the pudding with dairy-free chocolate chips and sliced almonds.
Refrigerate the pudding for at least 2 hours, or until it is chilled and set.
Serve the dairy-free chocolate almond milk pudding chilled and enjoy!

This creamy and indulgent pudding is perfect for satisfying your chocolate cravings while being dairy-free and vegan-friendly. Feel free to adjust the sweetness according to your preference.

Chocolate Banana Chia Seed Pudding Parfait

Ingredients:

For the chocolate chia seed pudding:

- 1 ripe banana
- 1 cup unsweetened almond milk (or any plant-based milk)
- 1/4 cup chia seeds
- 2 tablespoons cocoa powder
- 2 tablespoons maple syrup or agave syrup
- 1 teaspoon vanilla extract
- Pinch of salt

For assembling the parfait:

- Sliced bananas
- Granola or crushed nuts (optional)
- Fresh berries or other fruits for topping (optional)

Instructions:

In a blender, combine the ripe banana, almond milk, cocoa powder, maple syrup or agave syrup, vanilla extract, and a pinch of salt. Blend until smooth and well combined.

Transfer the mixture to a bowl or jar, and then stir in the chia seeds until evenly distributed.

Cover the bowl or jar and refrigerate for at least 4 hours or overnight, allowing the chia seeds to absorb the liquid and thicken to a pudding-like consistency.

Once the chocolate chia seed pudding has set, it's time to assemble the parfait. Start by spooning a layer of the chocolate chia seed pudding into serving glasses or jars.

Add a layer of sliced bananas on top of the pudding.

Repeat the layers until the glasses or jars are filled, ending with a layer of pudding on top.

Optionally, sprinkle some granola or crushed nuts on top of the final layer for added crunch and texture.

Garnish the parfaits with fresh berries or other fruits of your choice.

Serve immediately or refrigerate until ready to serve.

This Chocolate Banana Chia Seed Pudding Parfait is a nutritious and satisfying treat that's perfect for breakfast, snack, or dessert. Enjoy its creamy texture and rich chocolate flavor!

Vegan Chocolate Orange Cake

Ingredients:

For the cake:

- 2 cups all-purpose flour
- 1 cup granulated sugar
- 1/2 cup cocoa powder
- 1 teaspoon baking powder
- 1/2 teaspoon baking soda
- 1/2 teaspoon salt
- 1 cup freshly squeezed orange juice
- 1/2 cup unsweetened almond milk (or any plant-based milk)
- 1/2 cup vegetable oil
- 2 tablespoons apple cider vinegar
- Zest of 1 orange
- 1 teaspoon vanilla extract

For the chocolate orange ganache:

- 1/2 cup dairy-free chocolate chips
- 1/4 cup freshly squeezed orange juice
- Zest of 1 orange

For decoration (optional):

- Orange slices
- Orange zest
- Dairy-free chocolate shavings

Instructions:

Preheat your oven to 350°F (175°C). Grease and flour an 8-inch round cake pan or line it with parchment paper.
In a large mixing bowl, whisk together the flour, sugar, cocoa powder, baking powder, baking soda, and salt until well combined.
In a separate bowl, mix together the orange juice, almond milk, vegetable oil, apple cider vinegar, orange zest, and vanilla extract.

Pour the wet ingredients into the dry ingredients and mix until just combined. Be careful not to overmix.

Pour the batter into the prepared cake pan and smooth the top with a spatula.

Bake in the preheated oven for 30-35 minutes, or until a toothpick inserted into the center comes out clean.

Remove the cake from the oven and let it cool in the pan for 10 minutes before transferring it to a wire rack to cool completely.

While the cake is cooling, prepare the chocolate orange ganache. In a small saucepan, heat the orange juice over medium heat until it starts to simmer.

Remove from heat and add the chocolate chips and orange zest. Let it sit for a minute, then whisk until smooth and glossy.

Once the cake has cooled, pour the chocolate orange ganache over the top of the cake, allowing it to drip down the sides.

Optionally, decorate the cake with orange slices, orange zest, and dairy-free chocolate shavings.

Allow the ganache to set for a few minutes before slicing and serving.

Enjoy your Vegan Chocolate Orange Cake! It's moist, flavorful, and perfect for any occasion.

Dairy-Free Chocolate Peanut Butter Smoothie

Ingredients:

- 1 ripe banana, frozen
- 1 tablespoon cocoa powder
- 2 tablespoons natural peanut butter (make sure it's dairy-free)
- 1 cup unsweetened almond milk (or any other plant-based milk)
- 1 tablespoon maple syrup or agave syrup (optional, for added sweetness)
- Ice cubes (optional, for a colder smoothie)

Instructions:

Peel the ripe banana and slice it into chunks. Place the banana chunks in a blender.
Add the cocoa powder, natural peanut butter, unsweetened almond milk, and maple syrup or agave syrup (if using) to the blender.
If you prefer a colder smoothie, add a handful of ice cubes to the blender.
Blend all the ingredients until smooth and creamy. If the smoothie is too thick, you can add more almond milk to reach your desired consistency.
Once the smoothie is well blended and smooth, taste and adjust sweetness if necessary by adding more maple syrup or agave syrup.
Pour the dairy-free chocolate peanut butter smoothie into a glass.
Optionally, you can garnish the smoothie with a sprinkle of cocoa powder, a drizzle of peanut butter, or chopped peanuts for added texture.
Serve immediately and enjoy your creamy and indulgent dairy-free chocolate peanut butter smoothie!

This smoothie is perfect for breakfast, a post-workout snack, or a satisfying dessert. It's packed with flavor and nutrients, making it a delicious and healthy treat.

Chocolate Coconut Chia Seed Pudding

Ingredients:

- 1/4 cup chia seeds
- 1 cup coconut milk (canned, full-fat)
- 2 tablespoons cocoa powder
- 2 tablespoons maple syrup or agave syrup (adjust to taste)
- 1/2 teaspoon vanilla extract
- Shredded coconut, for garnish (optional)
- Chocolate shavings, for garnish (optional)
- Sliced strawberries, for garnish (optional)

Instructions:

In a mixing bowl, combine the chia seeds, coconut milk, cocoa powder, maple syrup or agave syrup, and vanilla extract. Stir well until all ingredients are thoroughly combined.
Let the mixture sit for a few minutes, then stir again to prevent clumping.
Cover the bowl and refrigerate the mixture for at least 2 hours or overnight, allowing the chia seeds to absorb the liquid and form a pudding-like consistency.
Once the chia seed pudding has set, give it a good stir.
Divide the pudding into serving cups or jars.
If desired, garnish the pudding with shredded coconut, chocolate shavings, and sliced strawberries.
Serve chilled and enjoy your delicious Chocolate Coconut Chia Seed Pudding!

This pudding makes for a nutritious and satisfying dessert or snack, packed with fiber, healthy fats, and antioxidants. It's also customizable, so feel free to adjust the sweetness and toppings to your liking.

Vegan Chocolate Black Bean Brownies

Ingredients:

- 1 can (15 oz) black beans, rinsed and drained
- 1/4 cup cocoa powder
- 1/2 cup maple syrup or agave syrup
- 1/4 cup coconut oil, melted
- 1 teaspoon vanilla extract
- 1/2 teaspoon baking powder
- Pinch of salt
- 1/4 cup dairy-free chocolate chips (optional)

Instructions:

Preheat your oven to 350°F (175°C). Grease or line an 8x8-inch baking pan with parchment paper.
In a food processor, combine the black beans, cocoa powder, maple syrup or agave syrup, melted coconut oil, vanilla extract, baking powder, and a pinch of salt. Blend until smooth and well combined, scraping down the sides of the food processor as needed.
If using, stir in the dairy-free chocolate chips into the batter.
Pour the batter into the prepared baking pan and spread it out evenly.
Bake in the preheated oven for 25-30 minutes, or until the brownies are set and a toothpick inserted into the center comes out clean.
Remove the brownies from the oven and let them cool in the pan for 10 minutes. Once cooled slightly, transfer the brownies to a wire rack to cool completely before slicing into squares.
Serve and enjoy your Vegan Chocolate Black Bean Brownies!

These brownies are fudgy, rich, and chocolatey, making them a delicious treat for vegans and non-vegans alike. They're also packed with protein and fiber from the black beans, making them a healthier alternative to traditional brownies.

www.ingramcontent.com/pod-product-compliance
Lightning Source LLC
LaVergne TN
LVHW061947070526
838199LV00060B/4013